What people are saying ab

Entre—PRAY—Neur

"Good practical wisdom from Pastor Vincent Broomfield. In *Entre—PRAY—neur* you will find yourself as to where you are and where you've always wanted to go. Let Pastor Broomfield take you on this journey."

Sam Chand, Leadership Consultant and
author of New Thinking—New Future
(www.samchand.com)

"*Entre—PRAY—neur* is a toolbox full of biblical principles that will help you grow your business by declaring the word. This book will be a great tool for marketplace ministry."

Pastor Jeremy Tuck

ENTRE—
PRAY—
NEUR

ENTRE—PRAY—NEUR

**DOING BUSINESS
GOD'S WAY.**

Vincent Broomfield

Scripture quotations marked KJV are taken from the King James Version of the Bible. Public domain. Scripture quotations marked NIV are taken from the Holy Bible, New International Version®, NIV®. Copyright © 1973, 1978, 1984, 2011 by Biblica, Inc.™ Used by permission of Zondervan. All rights reserved worldwide. www.zondervan.com. The "NIV" and "New International Version" are trademarks registered in the United States Patent and Trademark Office by Biblica, Inc.™ | Scripture quotations marked NKJV are taken from the New King James Version®. Copyright © 1982 by Thomas Nelson. Used by permission. All rights reserved. | Scripture quotations marked TLB are taken from The Living Bible copyright © 1971 by Tyndale House Foundation. Used by permission of Tyndale House Publishers Inc., Carol Stream, Illinois 60188. All rights reserved. The Living Bible, TLB, and The Living Bible logo are registered trademarks of Tyndale House Publishers. | Scripture quotations marked NLT are taken from the *Holy Bible*, New Living Translation, copyright © 1996, 2004, 2015 by Tyndale House Foundation. Used by permission of Tyndale House Publishers, Inc., Carol Stream, Illinois 60188. All rights reserved. | Scripture quotations marked MSG are taken from *THE MESSAGE*, copyright © 1993, 1994, 1995, 1996, 2000, 2001, 2002 by Eugene H. Peterson. Used by permission of NavPress. All rights reserved. Represented by Tyndale House Publishers, Inc. | Scripture quotations marked GNT are from the Good News Translation in Today's English Version—Second Edition. Copyright © 1992 by American Bible Society. Used by Permission.

For foreign and subsidiary rights, contact the author.

ISBN: 9781950718276   1 2 3 4 5 6 7 8 9 10

Printed in the United States of America

Entre—PRAY—neur
Definition

1. An Entre-PRAY-neur is an entrepreneur who follows the biblical principle of the written and verbal guidance of the Lord Jesus Christ in the operations of a self-developed and funded business.

2. It is a person or persons who have been given an idea or talent by God, and who will take the risk of trusting God in launching a business in the midst of a Christ-less world.

3. An Entre-PRAY-neur is a person or persons who grasp the whole idea of being the salt and light of the kingdom of God in a dark and clammy world and who share that light through business with all that is encountered.

Contents

    1. What is an Entre-PRAY-neur?
    2. What does being an Entre-PRAY-neur mean?
    3. What's the big idea of Entre-PRAY-neurship?

    1. Have your prayed? (hence Entre-PRAY-neur)
    2. Has God approved this move?
    3. Is this move within the plans of God?

    1. Talents
    2. No excuses
    3. Acknowledgement

    1. What's the point?
    2. Plan
    3. What's the foundation to success?

    1. Risk
    2. Fear
    3. Start

    1. Who's assigned to you during this season?
    2. Leadership
    3. Turn around and serve

Acknowledgements

I want to take this special moment to acknowledge a few people that has had a major impact in my life through support, love, and prayer. From the beginning of all time in my life my mother has been a great monument of support and love. I salute her for always being there no matter where there is.

I want to acknowledge and thank my wife for being such a grand pillar, lover, supporter, intercessor, and so much more in the years of transition that has gone on. Through her prayers and support we have been able to launch a ministry, raise great children, and share life together.

I take my hat off to the children of my life. The patients and love that the five of them has given is beyond the words of gratitude. I thank you for understanding the office time and quite space that I needed. I pray God's favor over your lives and continued blessing.

May this book be a starting place for all of you to see there is never a bearer in your life until you place one there. God has given us the tools to move forward in all things and He will never approve anything that He will not stand behind. Thank you all and lets enjoy the promises of God as He continues to reveal to us unlimited love and promises.

I want to give a great thanks to those who have been assigned to my life that has assisted me. Pastor Nathaniel Lee, Bishop Brian Keith Hodges, Apostle Jeremy Tuck, Dr. Sam Chand, and Dr. Chris Bowen thank you for your prayers and encouraging words.

Forward

It is my great honor to endorse this incredible book, "Entre—PRAY—neur". As both a business owner and minister of the Gospel, I believe this is a must-read for any Christian. Whether you have already started a business venture, or simply have a vision of launching out on your own in the future, this book will give you insight, clarity and the tools you need to assist you in finding true success that we all yearn for.

Through his writings, my friend, Vincent Broomfield, lays out the strategies of doing business God's way. When we live with integrity and obedience to His word in both our personal and professional lives, seeking His will above everything else to be done in and through us, we will indeed be on our way to prospering as our souls prosper.

Once we truly grasp the talents that God instilled within us and use them to serve both our Lord and others as He leads us, we can experience true success and genuine joy in our lives. When you find yourself doing what your Creator destined you to do, you'll never dread setting your alarm for the next morning.

It is my prayer that through this book, you, too, will find yourself #livingthedream!

Dr. Chris Bowen
DrChrisBowen.com
#LivingMyDream

Introduction

Proverbs 3:5-8 (NKJV)

⁵ Trust in the LORD with all your heart, And lean not on your own understanding; ⁶ In all your ways acknowledge Him, And He shall direct your paths. ⁷ Do not be wise in your own eyes; Fear the LORD and depart from evil. ⁸ It will be health to your flesh, And strength to your bones.

What is an Entre—PRAY—neur?

In the beginning of Genesis God told people to be fruitful and multiply (Genesis 1:28). Many people look at the Scripture from a viewpoint of sexuality, procreation, or simply getting some. That's the mind of the flesh. It's not wrong but it is not entirely true. According to Romans 8:5-7, the mind that is set on the flesh receives the things of the flesh which is death. The mind set on the spirit, however, receives the things of the spirit which is life. So, we must dig deeper into what God meant when he said be fruitful and multiply. My interpretation and understanding of that Scripture is to be fruitful in all things and multiply those things. To be fruitful means to produce a necessary thing and increase it.

Well your home and my home's necessary thing will be different. In this world money is a necessary thing. It is not, according to Matthew 6:24, supposed to be your God, but it is still necessary. We need it to pay mortgage, car notes, insurance, daycare, go shopping, and so much more. Being fruitful can also mean producing a home of peace, a marriage of trust, children of respect and honor. It is all based on what is the focal point of your life, house, and relationships.

The word multiply here according to Strong's concordance means to become many, become numerous, to grow great, to make large, increase. This is why some families have 13 children, other than the fact that there was not much distraction in the days of the procreated family, such as TV, social media, and other technology. The children begin to do that same in multiplying and making more babies. Proverbs 4:7 declares that "wisdom is the principal thing; Therefore, get wisdom. And in all your getting, get understanding." Simply put, get the wisdom but ensure that you understand the principle and why. So, in business or the start of one how do you take Scripture and apply it?

I know at this point you are wondering what is wrong with me and why I am trying to teach what is known. I would say to that, this is not the book for you at this time. I don't want to offend the person who already has the answers. I do, however, want to, under the leadership of the Holy Spirit, reverse the curse of Hosea 4:6. In Hosea 4:6 God made a statement that speaks to the ignorant, slaughtfulness, or just flat out unknown. He says in Hosea 4:6, "My people are destroyed for lack of knowledge. Because you have rejected knowledge, I also will reject you from being priest for Me." So many people in the world have found themselves lower in life than God intended because somewhere along the line they felt like they knew it all or were to prideful to get more. Proverbs 16:18 states that "pride goes before destruction, And a haughty spirit before a fall." So let's get into what this book is all about.

What does being an Entre—PRAY—neur mean?

Let me lay the foundation of what we will be discussing in the book. Entre-PRAY-Nuer is an entrepreneur who follows the biblical principle of the written and verbal guidance of the Lord Jesus Christ in the operations of a self-developed and funded business. Now I know you are saying there is no such word, nor do I see that in the Bible. One of the things that I have been able to appreciate about the creation of God, mankind, is the fact that He gave us dominion and intellect. All of the words in the dictionary were created by man. I mean before the 90's the word can't was not in the dictionary. I know because for the first part of my life while I was in my academic beginnings, I used the word can't a lot. I used it because of my environmental dialect, culture, and the simple fact that I wanted to give my English teacher a hard time.

I felt I could not because I didn't know that I could, until someone not only told me but took the time to develop and show me. Honestly in the frame of time I really felt in so many ways that I could not do. Throughout the years of my life and the people I have been able to encounter I have found that I can. So, I look forward to the day that Entre-PRAY-Neur becomes a dictionary word. It will come to mean 1. An entrepreneur who follows the biblical principle of the written and verbal guidance of the Lord Jesus Christ in the operations of a self-developed and funded business. 2. A person or persons who have been given an idea or talent by God, and who will take the risk of trusting God in launching a business in the midst of a Christ-less world. 3. A person or persons who grasp the whole idea of being the salt and light of the kingdom of God in a dark and clammy world and who share that light through business with all that is encountered.

What's the big idea of Entre—PRAY—neurship?

As a Christian, one who follows the Lord Jesus Christ and is obedient to the commands that He has left behind for us to follow, it must be done in all facets of life. In the home, on the job, as a parent, as an employee, and as a CEO. Jesus said in John 14:15, "If you love Me, keep My commandments." In fact, as He was instructing His disciples at the time, a naysayer, I mean a bystander, a Pharisee in Mathew 22:36, a lawyer asked "Teacher, which is the greatest commandment in the law?" Of course, we know he was testing Jesus trying to get Jesus to say something that would incriminate Himself. In verses 37-39 Jesus said to him, "You shall love the LORD your God with all your heart, with all your soul, and with all your mind. This is the first and great commandment. And the second is like it: 'You shall love your neighbor as yourself'" (emphasis added).

In this section of Scripture, we see that Jesus challenges us not to just say we love Him but show that we love Him by obeying His commands. In Mathew 5:13-16 Jesus commanded us to be the salt of the earth that preserves and to be the light of the world that is not hidden but shines. Then we see that one of the greatest commands tells us to love our neighbor. As the fore mentioned Christian in the various parts of the world in life we are commanded to be examples of Jesus in the world. This is not going to be an easy task as we must do this in a world that is filled with darkness and selfishness.

So, what is the big idea of Entre-PRAY-neurship? It is being a businessman or woman of creation who has built their vision and mission off of the principles of Scripture. As we have seen, being a Christian does not mean being one only at church or for church. It does not mean that we are hypocritical and wear one coat around likeminded people and another when we are not. I recently have had the ability to assist a client/friend with the purchase of land and right after we began to interview contractors to do work for him that would be detailed and rigorous work. One of the first things that we agreed on is that the contractor had to be a man or woman of faith.

This was said because as men and women of faith we are saying that we are Christians and we will operate our business by faith, integrity, and love. Unfortunately, this is not what we received. This further aroused my disappointment as it relates to being a man or woman of God doing business in a world that encounters believers and unbelievers. Now let me say this with a disclaimer. I have in my lifetime owned numerous businesses and I have not in all of this timeframe been a man of integrity and faith. I have in some areas consciously done wrong. Over time and with more study of God's Word and building a better relationship with Jesus Christ I have found that by doing God's children wrong we become enemies with God. Psalm 105:15 says, "Do not touch My anointed ones (someone who has been consecrated and sanctified), And do My prophets (spokesman, mouthpiece) no harm" (emphasis added). By doing them right we open up the floodgates of blessings over our life and business.

Once I became more familiar with the Word of God and began to reflect and see how I feel when someone takes advantage of me, I've allowed the Holy Spirit to show me how at times I took advantage of others. As a man of faith, a man of God, this is absolutely out of line. So what's the whole idea of Entre-PRAY-neurship? It's being a true man or woman of faith living in true integrity and doing what Colossians tells us to do and that's to do everything according to God.

This means that when we develop plans for the business, we take into consideration that we will encounter God's great people. That's right. God's GREAT people. I know, I know. Sometimes they just get on the last nerve. The narrative when God came to Solomon and said, "I am proud of you. Ask me anything and I will do it for you." Solomon replied, "Give me the wisdom to deal with your GREAT people" (paraphrased).

I believe if we ask God to do the same with us, we will be able to accomplish two goals as Christians: 1. Share the gospel of Jesus Christ and not only how great He is but how He can change a life and make it 1,000 times better. 2. Provide for our families through making money and be prosperous in the things that God has promised. This is by the way my opinion the reason the world is the way it is today, because the body of Christ, His disciples, are not being obedient to His commands.

What Does God Say?
Chapter 1

Proverbs 3:5, 6 (NKJV)

⁵ Trust in the LORD with all your heart, And lean not on your own understanding; ⁶ In all your ways acknowledge Him, And He shall direct your paths.

Ephesians 6:18 (NKJV)

¹⁸ praying always with all prayer and supplication in the Spirit, being watchful to this end with all perseverance and supplication for all the saints.

How, God, oh how will I do this? How, dear Lord, will I be able to pull this off? Guide my thought, my hands, and my feet Lord to do your will. If only this was the prayer of so many men and women of faith. Those whom claim to be a child of God, a royal priesthood, one saved by Christ. So many times in my life I have walked into an establishment knowing that the owners are Christians and then realize they are Sunday-only Christians. The Christians who put on a holy face on Sunday and put on the flesh when they leave church.

God asked a question of who would go, whom He could send. Isaiah answered and said, "Send me. I will go." Are there any "send me; I will go" men or women of faith? I answer my own question by saying yes there are. They are there and they have the heart of God. The problem with the moral balance between the world and the Word is the time spent with God. Every Christian who is a proclaimed child of God deals with the temptations of life on a regular basis and has not been taught how to effectively carry the torch and be the light.

My response to this is we must seek the face of God to really get instructions on what we have heard. Samuel heard the voice of God call him multiple times and ran to the man over him, not knowing it was not him who called. It was the Lord calling him to the next level of his life. Often times we have heard a voice and not sure who it was and we ignored it or because of fear ran from it back into the world that we have known for centuries. This unbalanced conundrum has us looking as if we really do not love God. We look like the so called Christians acting one way on Sunday and another on Monday. Sure there are those whom you must continue to pray for, but you are not they.

You heard right. God has put something way down on the inside of you that He wants to mature that He is now calling you to launch in the business world or at least rehab the one you currently own to look like the kingdom business that it was created to be. How do we as men and women of faith transition from the old man to the new man? A hard task that if you are confused or lost becomes harder. Would you say that because you are a believer that you pray? If not, that's ok. Everyone's prayer life is different in the stages and growth than the other. Prayer, I will tell you, is and should be the foundation of your life.

When you build a house you do not ever put the frame up first or install the lawn, bushes, and flowers. No, that is crazy. So the same with the business you are launching, will launch, or are in the middle of launching already, has to be strategically planned in order for it to be right. In planning anything, no matter what it is that you are seeking to do, you always have the first step.

What Does God Say?

The first step in this case of being an Entre-PRAY-neur is prayer. Pray first, move last, is the model of ministry. Even if God has already confirmed your move, now you must ask how, when, where. The question to you is in this burning you have in your heart to launch a business God's way, have you prayed about it?

Have You Prayed About This?

Prayer is the pathway to enter God's presence to get your direction for the day, the month, the year. In your life, your marriage, your family, your business have you prayed about it? Proverbs 3:5 tells us to trust in the Lord in everything. Verse six guides us to acknowledge God in everything and God will direct our path. Have you prayed about this? To start a business especially God's way will take time to strategize and execute. But if it is God's business shouldn't you get your direction from God on how to do the business, deal with His great people, ensure that the business is also ministry in God's eyes?

See, in everything we do, we want to do it all onto God. Well, if you are doing something for me, unless it is a surprise, should you come to me to get instructions on how I want it done? Then you can execute the movement of carrying out the task. I believe this is why so many Christian owned business are failures so dramatically because, the owner, a fleshly man or woman, is doing it their way instead of God's.

You will not always get the answer you want, by the way, when you pray and ask God. See, the reason we pray is to get the what, when, where, why, and how. These are the marching orders to carry out the mission. When God called Joshua, God gave him detailed instructions on what to do in order to accomplish the goal. During the journey of conquering the land when a step was missed because of disobedience, then there was a moment of pain. The step was missed not because God did not say the what, when, where, why, and how but because the man who stole the items that belonged to God wanted to do things his way. This caused terrible ripples to begin in the Israelites and soldier was lost.

There is a reason that throughout the Bible prayer is spoken about more than most things. God wants to be part of what you are doing. In fact, if God has initiated the task, why would you give regular updates and ask for assistance when you have hit a wall that you cannot navigate? You must take this startup to God. God has to direct your path.

Second Chronicles 7:14 tells us the formula to getting in God's presence and getting our land healed. Our land of course being whatever God has directed us to go and conquer. The land of marriage, the land of ministry, the land of business, the land of finances. This Scripture mentioned is God himself speaking and He says:

> *2 Chronicles 7:14 (NLT)*
> *14 Then if my people who are called by my name will humble themselves and pray and seek my face and turn from their wicked ways, I will hear from heaven and will forgive their sins and restore their land.*

In this formula we see pray and seek. Both of them involve talking to God and being in His presence. Have you prayed and asked God what He wants you to do in the business? Another Scripture that supports praying for direction is:

Philippians 4:13 (NKJV)
¹³ I can do all things <u>through</u> Christ who strengthens me.

Yes, you can do all thing THROUGH Christ Jesus. This "can do all things" to me means that it will happen and I will not fail. Whereas I can do it on my own but I may find myself up and down with emotions and chaos. It is in the "through" that we see the need to pray for your business. You must always funnel your thoughts and actions through Christ to see if they match up to God's approval. Really! Has God approved this startup or are you taking on a journey that really is a distraction to what God truly has for you?

Has God Approved This Startup?

Surely if we are going to go to God in prayer for the what, when, where, why, and how then we will be obedient to God. He is the creator, the beginning and the end, alpha and omega. I'm just saying. Surely you will not bow down on your knees, pray, and ask God for direction and God tells you what He wants and then you get up and do the very opposite.

Okay Jonah, because of your disobedience you are about to cause pain about yourself and so many around you because you won't follow the approval or disapproval of God. See, Jonah didn't want to do it because he knew that the people would truly have ears to hear and do what God says through him. So therefore Jonah went on the run as if God was not Omnipresent (everywhere at the same time). Jonah caused merchants to lose their product and a ship crew to almost lose their ship, product, and lives.

Don't be the business owner, Entre-PRAY-neur, who talks to God and then turns and does things your way anyway. Don't be the man or woman of faith who goes only to inform what you are going to do. How disrespectful can you be? You open business to provide a service or product. Now God is using that in order to allow you to connect with His great people in order for you to influence them to come back to Him, stay with Him.

When you get into prayer, ensure that you stay there until you have heard the voice of God and the right instructions to what God wants. Once you have completed your prayer, if you have not heard God's answer, then do not move forward with business until you have. God is able to confirm His answer through a prophet, your pastor, or just someone whom God knows you will listen to.

Once God confirms then move or not. In the writing of this book I had felt that it was time to begin to write it or one of the other ones that is in my heart, but I was not going to move until I heard from God. So I began to pray about it and as I prayed I felt peace about the book. Peace, by the way, is a strong indication that God approves. But then I still did not move until I knew for sure that this is what God wanted and not me. See, if God approves it then He will supply it.

It was maybe a few days later that a mentor-friend was over to the house and in the middle of conversation she began to share God's voice with me. She never knew, in fact no one at this point even knew, that I was thinking about it but God. She started to proclaim that she saw a writer in me and then began to name subject matters of books. On the inside I was shouting and screaming all at the same time!

Now I know it is true God wants me to move forward. As if I don't already have enough on my plate. I had never written in this manner before. What, where, when, why, and most importantly from someone who was afraid of how! This is what I was screaming on the inside but not wanting to show weakness to my family and friend.

Months had gone by and I went to go and support my wife who was on assignment to preach when God spoke to me again and confirmed the book writing. Now I was certain and secure that it is time. So I began to pray about each chapter title and subject. How would I assist you, God's great man, God's great woman, to be successful in starting and sustaining a business God's way?

Now that I know God approves, is it the right season? When exactly does God want me to carry the task out? Is this startup within the season and plans of God?

Is This Startup Within the Season and Plans of God?

Okay, we now know that God approves, but when is the deadline to make this vision a reality? Are you supposed to start now? Are you supposed to just begin to research now? Do you already know how to do it but you just want to ensure if it is for this window of opportunity or the next? It very well may be months to years before God fires the gun to start the race. You know you're a runner but you can't start running until the gun fires.

Your prayer time with God now has to change in conversation. When, God? And what exactly are the details to accomplishing this Your way and not mine? This is the time of prayer that you are simply listening and not talking. We talk so much that when something is being said we miss it entirely because we are speaking the same time God is. Your next step is to listen to understand and not to reply.

Now is the time to purchase some type of writing pad or journal to begin to capture what it is that God has in His plan for the business you will start. What are the demographics of God's plan? This may not be smart business to start a Starbucks in the middle of an impoverished area. Financially, in an impoverished area the marketing reviews and reports may not support this as the place to start. God, on the other hand, may say this is where He wants it to be.

Now you have to fight the corporate executives on putting a franchise in this area. This being an opinioned scenario means that God may have you go against the grain of what is normal in the world. If God called you to it God will guide you through it. You can't see what God is doing in the future. This was a problem for the majority of the Israelites receiving the report of the promised land when the spies returned.

Second Corinthians 5:7 explains that as Christians we are to walk by faith and not by sight. It will not always look the way you think it should. You have a time limit to what you desire but God is not bound by time. Your job is to be obedient. God will cause the time and normality of things to shift in your favor.

Faith is the fuel that will cause this vehicle of business not only to move but to be successful. Surround yourself with praying, faithful Christians. Have faith that God knows what He is doing in calling you to achieve a task even if you don't have faith in yourself. He KNOWS the plans that He has for you and HE knew you even when you before you were in the womb. He knows the season and task that He, God, wants you to do. Seek God's face and as you listen to His guidance, walk by faith. If you don't know where to start or what to do, don't move until you hear God.

PRINCIPLE:

Always know what it is that God wants.

APPLICATION:

Intentionally labor in prayer and fasting to get what it is God has.

PRAYER:

Lord Jesus, I pray for the man or the woman reading this book right now. I pray that you, Lord, will be their absolute guide to doing business your way. I ask in Jesus' name that you will provide for them all the date, the money, the time that is needed for them to accomplish the vision you have given them. When the doubt sets in God, I pray that you will do a clean sweep immediately and restore their faith. We ask these things in your mighty name. Amen.

What's in Your Hand?
Chapter 2

Exodus 4:2(NLT)
2 Then the LORD asked him, "What is that in your hand?" "A shepherd's staff," Moses replied.

Proverbs 18:16(NKJV)
16 A man's gift makes room for him, And brings him before great men.

Years ago, when I was the manager of a multi-family complex, I encountered a young lady who was just going through the ringer. Man, she was catching it left and right. She was a single mother of two and had just been laid off from her job. She had a little money put away but not much. So, for a couple months she was able to handle her rent, but it got to a point that she was just out. Between the kids and the regular bills, the money was slipping through her fingers fast. So, she started to come to the office to speak with my assistant to work out getting her rent paid over a few weeks or so.

Eventually she and the assistant fell into a dispute and the assistant added her to the list of evictions. Now it was on my desk and I was going through the list, researching the history of payments and making calls. Now after digging into about six months' worth of ledgers for this particular resident I saw that up until about 3 months prior she had never been late and was a resident of the property for over five years. So, I gave her a call and set an appointment for her to come in and speak with me.

As the knock came to my door, "Your appointment is here," I looked out the window into the lobby and recognized the lady. This is the young lady who not only paid her rent on time but paid her rent beforehand. I say to myself, I have sent her multiple $50 discount cards because she is always on time. Thinking out loud to myself at the time, What the hell? So, I went out and greeted her and invited her in my office. As I watched her gather her children, I could see her brokenness and worry.

We talked for a while trying to figure out a strategy on getting her rent paid and caught up. The Spirit of God placed on my heart to ask her what it was that she liked to do. She paused for a minute and before she could say anything I asked, "In your days of good and when you were just sitting around with no worries and loving life, what do you like to do?" She again took a minute to think and said she liked to bake. This was right up my alley as I am a big sweets person.

So I mentioned to her that I was a man of God and that I wanted to ask her to do me a favor that I believed would help her. She reluctantly said okay and I could see on her face that the worry of her rent was more important. So I said to her, "Don't worry. I am going somewhere with this that will assist you in paying your rent." I proceeded to say that our corporate office had multiple meetings a week and that my wife and I purchased a cake at least every two weeks. So I said to her that if I could help her sell the cakes, would she bake them so that she could make the money?

Of course, she was thinking, "I am not about to waste my money baking cakes that might not get sold." She was not a business-minded person at the time. She was more of a "go to work, make the money, have a 401k, and go home" person. So

I helped her understand that if she took about $50 and purchased the product to make five cakes and sold each one for about $35 she could multiply her money. Now at that point she was in wonder.

Story short, so we can get to the purpose of this chapter. She was able to begin selling cakes and pies and start paying on her rent. She eventually learned how to register a business and come up with a plan to make money from the very thing she liked doing anyway. Last I spoke with someone who knew her, she owned a cupcake store.

TALENTS/GIFTS

So I have to ask the person who is reading this book who may be saying, "Okay, yea, yea. But what does that have to do with me? I don't have a skill." In Romans 12:6-8(NIRV)it says, "We all have gifts. They differ according to the grace God has given to each of us. Do you have the gift of prophecy? Then use it according to the faith you have. If your gift is serving, then serve. If it is teaching, then teach. Is it encouraging others? Then encourage them. Is it giving to others? Then give freely. Is it being a leader? Then work hard at it. Is it showing mercy? Then do it cheerfully."

When God created you, He was very particular in what He was doing and why. In Jeremiah 29:11 God says, "I know the plans that I have for you." Why would God give everyone else a gift but you? Majority of the time the gift that God has given us is the very thing that we do on a regular basis and call it a hobby or pastime. Many times, this very thing is what we discount and look over. It is, however, the thing that God is going to use to bless your soul. Let's look at 2 Kings 4.

2 Kings 4:1-38(NLT)

⁴One day the widow of a member of the group of prophets came to Elisha and cried out, "My husband who served you is dead, and you know how he feared the Lord. But now a creditor has come, threatening to take my two sons as slaves." ² "What can I do to help you?" Elisha asked. "Tell me, what do you have in the house?" "Nothing at all, except a flask of olive oil," (italics added) she replied. ³ And Elisha said, "Borrow as many empty jars as you can from your friends and neighbors. ⁴ Then go into your house with your sons and shut the door behind you. Pour olive oil from your flask into the jars, setting each one aside when it is filled." ⁵ So she did as she was told. Her sons kept bringing jars to her, and she filled one after another. ⁶ Soon every container was full to the brim! "Bring me another jar," she said to one of her sons. "There aren't any more!" he told her. And then the olive oil stopped flowing.⁷ When she told the man of God what had happened, he said to her, "Now sell the olive oil and pay your debts, and you and your sons can live on what is left over."

As we see, the widow did the very thing that so many others do. The very thing that God used to bless her house for a lifetime is the very thing that she discounted. I ask you, what is it that you are discounting in your life that God has purposed to bless your life?

What is in your hand? Not physically but spiritually. What talent has God given and graced you with that with some mentoring and leadership could change the trajectory of your WHOLE life? I say WHOLE life because it is not just about you. In the Scripture above we see that after the widow and her sons were obedient to the voice of God that came through

What's in Your Hand?

the man of God they were blessed from the widow to her sons. This speaks to the generational wealth.

> [7] *When she told the man of God what had happened, he said to her, "Now sell the olive oil and pay your debts, and you and your sons can live on what is left over."*

We as the children of God who have been chosen and made royal must understand that God's plans for us are not just to fulfill our hearts' desire but to care and provide for a bloodline.

No Excuses!

The widow initially responded with, *"Nothing at all, except a flask of olive oil,"*. This comment made me think of the man at the pool of Bethesda who had excuses for why he was not healed and who did what Adam did in the beginning, blamed it on the fact that no one would help him get in the pool (John 5:1-15).

What excuses are you coming up with and why? I can't answer the what, but I can give the why a shot. Many of you have been told throughout your life that you were only made to do one thing. So as your life went forward and you began to live what they said you became comfortable. Even in your comfort of having a home, money, and a family you still don't have peace. This is because you were created for so much more. Your ministry assignment is a business that will bless so many.

You have to get out of your way by getting rid of the excuses. See, as men and women of God we must walk by faith and not by sight. Of course, not everyone is graced for business. If they were, the world would be unbalanced. If you have this

Entre—PRAY—neur

book in your hand either by choice or someone gave it to you, that's because God has graced you for it. You must defeat the demon of excuses. First way to do that is to find like-minded people and start a small group to discuss the steps to start with. Business is not easy but it's not hard either.

God has assigned someone to assist you in jumping, getting out of the boat (Peter), taking the risk, and becoming a vessel used by God. In Exodus chapter 3 when God called Moses to go and tell Pharaoh to let His people go, Moses began to come up with all the excuses he could. One of them was that he could not speak, but God told him that he would have Aaron, Moses's brother, speak for him.

God already knows what you need and who you need in your life to help you. I encourage you to pray and seek God's face and direction as to whom He has chosen for you.

You Have What It Takes.

Whether you have become an expert in your hobby or not you have what it takes. Whether you know business or not, you have what it takes. Nothing comes overnight. It takes time and experience to master anything. So I am here to tell you, you have what it takes. Surround yourself with people who will encourage you and help shape you into the Entre-PRAY-neur God has created you to be. We will talk about connections in a later chapter.

That does not mean get rid of the people who doubt you. I believe that those people are necessary. In Psalm 23 God says that He will prepare a table in the presence of your enemy, so jump all in and get your talent and gifts ready for God to use you in the world to bless someone. Many books like this one have been written to assist you in launching off into the deep, but you have to have the courage to get out of the boat.

Your skill has already been established in your hobby or pastime. Some haven't really thought about what it is that God has gifted them to do. Once you have acknowledged what that skill or gift that God has given you is then you can get into what it will take to launch that gift into the world.

Yes, once you have developed the business you will have to run it like a business and not a hobby, but as long as you love what you do you will never work a day in your life. You have what it takes. Begin to brainstorm now how to monetize the hobby or gift the Lord has given you and go all in, because

YOU HAVE WHAT IT TAKES!

Suggested Books:
- Never Chase a Paycheck Again Dr. Robert Watkin
- Soar!! Bishop T.D. Jakes
- Why Business Matters To God Van Duzer
- If It Ain't Broke, Break It Dr. Chris Bowen
- Failure: The Womb of Success Dr. Sam Chand

Suggested Startups:

Interior Home Design	Book Writing
Lawn Care	Barbershop
Mobile Car Wash	T-shirts
Mobile Mechanic	Trucking Business
Song Writing	Real Estate Investing
Catering	Graphic Design

PRINCIPLE:

Know the worth of your gift.

APPLICATION:

Sharpen the gift and use your tool well.

PRAYER:

Lord Jesus, I pray for the man or the woman reading this book right now. I pray that you will open their minds to the gift that you have put in their hands. Allow them to see, Lord, what you have given them and teach them how to use the gift for your kingdom. In Your name. Amen.

Pave the Path
Chapter 3

Habakkuk 2:2, 3

² Then the Lord answered me and said: "Write the vision And make it plain on tablets, That he may run who reads it. ³ For the vision is yet for an appointed time; But at the end it will speak, and it will not lie. Though it tarries, wait for it; Because it will surely come, It will not tarry.

In secondary school it was always customary for the English teacher to ensure that in your writing or reading that you ask the questions: What? When? Why? Who? Where? and How? In this topic of writing this way of thinking and questioning is as well appropriate. The big question is why? Why are you doing what you're doing? What is the pathway to get to the finish line in your kingdom-driven business? Has this pathway already been paved or are you paving it yourself? If it has already been paved, who paved it and are they accessible to help you navigate it?

Before the subject is spoken about further, let's deal with some things. We have touched already and will touch more in chapter five about who has been assigned to help you. It is, however, important for you to understand that if there has been someone in front of you who has already paved the pathway for you to get where you are going, don't repave it. There may be some areas for you to patch, but if there is nothing that you are making better don't interrupt the system that has already been put in place.

The system put in place has a vision attached to it that can assist you in how to get where you are going. A system or vision. The vision is the map of where you are going. What does the finish line look like? This is the best place to start in your paving. You can't get where you are going if you don't know where that is. To pave the path, you must first know what the path is supposed to look like, what direction it is supposed to go in, who will use the path, and more importantly how you are going to pave it—financially, that is.

While in the U.S. Army we were given the skill set of navigating through a terrain that may be unfamiliar to us. In this instruction, we were encouraged to do it alone first and then as a team. While doing it alone you had to first identify your current place and then what direction you were headed. If you started off in the wrong direction it is going to discourage you once you finally come to the understanding of where you are and how far off the path you have gone. This is not a thumbs to quite. No, this just means you have that much more work and grind to do to get caught up.

Disclaimer: In the time that I was in the military we used paper maps to determine where we are and where we were going. So for this discussion on paving the pathway we are going to use this though process.

Now once you received your map you would first get your bearings and figure out which way is true north. By finding true north you can then identify your starting point. We all must have a starting point in business. Are you financially funded already? Are you absolutely broke? Do you have assets that you can leverage? Is there someone in your sphere of influence that you can get to invest? Do you have a good reputation for them to invest in? What does your credit score look like? Can you go to a bank to get your financial startup?

Again not to discourage you but to ensure that the materials to pave that pathway have been outlined and taken into consideration. This journey is not a quick and fast, start to finish in a day journey. The pathway is not one mile long. Your mind set in the start will determine the celebration in the finish.

What's the Point?

What is your starting point? This was one of my absolute failures in business over the years. I always thought if you had an idea you pray about it and God will make it happen. I was way off base. Faith without works is dead. You have to have a starting point financially in order to ensure that your business has a great take off and is successful in flight.

One of the areas to focus on is why are you starting this business? You should only start a business for one or two reasons: 1. To will it to your family. Are you planning to leave this business as part of your legacy? Will this business be set up to take care of your kids' kids when they go to college and start off life? Proverbs 13:2 says," A good man leaves an inheritance to his children's children." Is this the vision that God has given you? or 2. Start a business to sell.

I have been in Real Estate for over 20 years now and along the way I have been able to experience multiple things. One of them has been that you can sell a business like you sell a home. There are business brokers who specialize in assisting corporations, big or small, to sell their company. It is very lucrative by the way.

After exiting out of the active military I started a business installing car stereos and window tint. During the time that I was in business I became an authorized dealer for a company called Primeco. It was a prepaid mobile phone company. Primeco Personal Communications, L.P. was a collaboration of Bell Atlantic, Nynex, US West, and AirTouch Communications.

Primeco was acknowledged as the largest wireless phone service launch in U.S. History. In January 1999 AirTouch received purchase offers from Bell Atlantic, MCI, and Vodafone. Vodafone's offer was accepted and they merged with AirTouch the same month. Bell Atlantic approached Vodafone Airtouch about merging all three wireless operations later in the same year. So Bell Atlantic Mobile, AirTouch, and Primeco entered into a joint venture to be called Verizon Wireless as we know it today.

I haven't researched to see what the total buy number was during that time, but I do know that Verizon has built a marketing to be the largest mobile company with cell towers everywhere. So as you see what you start off as small can become eye candy to someone who has a vision to grow large. In 2015 I started working in the I.T. department with a company that was named XPO, but it had just purchased a smaller company called 3D. The vision for XPO was to acquire multiple smaller companies that would take on their name and make them the largest logistic company worldwide.

Now what's the point? Why are you starting the business? Now that God has given you direction to what, when, where, who, and how, what's the outcome? Can you see the end? Now that you can see the end and what direction is needed to get there, what's the plan?

What's The Plan?

How are you going to effectively pull this off? In the Scripture written in Habakkuk 2:2 it says write the vision and make it plain. Making it plain means to be clear in the details of execution. Every company has SOP or standard operating procedures. This SOP is compiled with information on how to handle certain tasks the company's way. Of course, each company is going to be completely different in operation. But is there a mentor who can assist you with the framework of the plan?

I say framework because the reality is that this SOP will be changed multiple times throughout the pathway of business. It will be changed because you, the company, the people your hire will change it. So start with a framework of how you want things to go. Don't let anyone dismantle your framework. They can add to it but they cannot take away from it. This is the reason why you start you planning with a focus group or interest meeting.

The meeting is built with like-minded people who have your vision in mind and will help you write the plan. Build the meeting with people who may not be on your team but have experience in the areas that will help pave your path. Some may have marketing field experience, some technical experience, accounting experience, and much more. It is imperative that you write out your outline of needs. By doing so you are able to go in prayer and allow the Holy Spirit to guide your footsteps to the right person(s).

Remember that being an Entre-PRAY-neur means that nowhere along the way can you leave out prayer. So let it be known that every step of this process has to start and end with prayer.

Now that you have gathered the focus group your task will be to keep them on task. This is your company and you have brought them in for insight. You are in the data gathering stage and you don't want to move beyond this stage faster then necessary.

Who is going to be your target audience? For your product or services who exactly does God what you to target? Your plan has to include them because they are the ones that God has assigned you to. Remember in this thing called business you want to make a profit. This profit, however, cannot be your god or your business will FAIL!

Luke 16:13 (NLT)
[13] "No one can serve two masters. For you will hate one and love the other; you will be devoted to one and despise the other. You cannot serve God and be enslaved to money."

What's the foundation to success?

The foundation to success is your mission. The mission is the absolute slab to build the house called a business on. I was able to work for Chick-fil-A for a couple of years at the corporate office. In the front of the office there is a monument that shows the company's mission. I don't remember it word for word but I do remember that it says something in the way of taking care of God's people.

The saying "It is not how you start but how you finish" is a great saying. I do get where the saying is coming from. If you start slow you can always finish stronger and faster once you get your rhythm. But in the line of building a house if you don't build the foundation right at the start, your finish will be terrible.

Jesus told a parable about a man building a house on sand versus rock. The outcome of building on sand is when a storm comes through and rocks your house (business), it will not stand.

So what's the rock in your foundation? What is the mission in your business? Each one is going to be different. God has the big picture of what He is looking for in the lives of His children. Who needs what and when they need it. Who is He going to use to help the one who needs help? Well in your mission development hear the voice of God to get your foundational mission. Are you going to be assigned to the weakest economic area? Will you cover the next generation or your generation? Is there a particular focus on the generation to what your vision is? What are the marching orders to get to the finish line with so many of God's children in tow? A mission statement is a sentence describing a company's function, markets, and competitive advantages; a short, written statement of your business goals and philosophies. A mission statement defines what an organization is, why it exists, its reason for being.

PRINCIPLE:
Write the vision.

APPLICATION:
Strategize and execute God's plan.

PRAYER:
Lord Jesus, I pray for the man or the woman reading this book right now. I pray that you will give them the strength to pave the path you have assigned them too. Give them the boldness to get out of the fear boat. Give them the boldness to walk with clarity and confidence. I

declare that eyes have not seen nor ears heard the things that you will complete in and through their hands. In your name. Amen.

Ready, Set, Jump!
Chapter 4

Matthew 14:28
²⁸ And Peter answered Him and said, "Lord, if it is You, command me to come to You on the water."

2 Timothy 1:7
⁷ For God has not given us a spirit of fear, but of power and of love and of a sound mind.

One of my favorite sports while I was in high school was track. I loved track because it was a group event that individuals could conquer by themselves. Now don't get me misunderstood. I am a team player, but sometimes some things have to be done alone. Everyone does not have the skill that you do. Until you are able to master your skill, it is hard to become a part of a team.

You don't want to drag them down while you figure yourself out. So as a track runner you get in your own cloud and find your own rhythm and run. In the beginning of a race each runner finds their individual starting block and they prepare for what's ahead. They are mentally preparing each phase of this run: who is their competition and what is it that they have against them.

In fact, some begin to even talk themselves out of the win. They do so by worrying about if they are good enough or if they will be able to keep up. One of my coaches during this time of track told me that you won't know your strength until you walk in it. For a very long time I had absolutely no idea of what that meant. Why are you even saying it to me right now? Do you not see my competition? They are going to leave me.

My first long distance race ever was the 4x4: one time around the track as fast as you could. Not taking into consideration what I had been through in my life and the fact that I ran almost everywhere. I ran to school, I would run to my brother's house, I would run to visit my girlfriend. I grew up running.

In my running I would find the rhythm of my feet slapping the ground and I would make a song to it or I would develop a beat. This song and beat diverted my mind to a different space and before I knew it two, three, eight miles later I was at my destination.

So here we are in the blocks and the voice shouts Ready! Set! Go! Then five to six men or women take off in the unknown of who will be the winner today. Who would make it around this track without injury? Who would come in first, second, and third? Will it be me?

I found myself doing what I always have done and that's finding my rhythm and singing my song. I drifted off into my own little world, not seeing anyone in front of me and really not worrying about where they were behind me. Yea, I knew that someone was going to pass me up. I just knew it. It was just a matter of time before I would see swinging hands or tapping feet with their own little rhythm passing me.

Now we are at our last curve and I feel this extra push as I realize I am still in the front. Not sure how far behind me anyone is. I mean it is a competition and I know there is someone out there just as good as I am. I don't see them, though.

Where are they? So I decided on this last leg I was going to put everything on the table. All the energy I could develop. All the strength I could gather. I was going to run until I was 20 yards past the finish line.

So I shouted Ready! Set! Go! Yes, in the middle of the race I started all over again. I found the strength to fire my own gun and start a new race. Between me and self I raced and when I crossed the finish line and came to know where I was, I was turning another corner. This race was over, and I was past the finish line. I conquered all the doubts and fears. I took this risk even though I decided that I would not be able to do it.

As I stopped and turned around, my coach and teammates were running to me in excitement and dismay. I had broken a 4x4 record at the school and didn't even realize it. Forty-three seconds is what it took me to run around that track one time as fast as I could that day. I never thought I would be able to compete let alone win, let alone break a record. In fact, I still was not sure what that meant.

Take the Risk

Often times in a person's life the main obstacle that he or she has to overcome is the reality of self. We talk ourselves out of the blessings that God has for us. I would encourage you to take the risk. You will never know what you can do until you do it. You will never know how far you can go until you try it. Take the risk. Yes, it looks scary and you doubt what you can do.

In Matthew 14 Jesus had just finished blessing the people of God teaching them biblical principles of life. It became late and Jesus told His disciples to get in the boat and go to the other side of the river. Now in this narrative Jesus did not start off in the boat with them. So the disciples were obedient to Christ and they left. As they were in the boat midway to the other side a great wind arose and begin to toss the boat.

While the boat was being tossed, they saw a figure's shadow on the water coming toward them. The disciples became afraid and worry set in. Then Christ called out and told them not to be afraid for it was Him. Peter recognized His voice and made one of the biggest power steps ever. He said, "Jesus, if that is you, command me to come out on the water."

Now what person in his or her right mind would think enough to open their mouth and say such a thing? First of all, a person would naturally think, "Hey, we can't walk on water!" Not Peter. Peter took the risk and opened his mouth. Let me tell you: be careful what you ask for. The Word of God declares that we have the power in our mouth to cause death or life to happen and be manifested upon us. So Jesus told Peter to come and history was written. Jesus and Peter walked on water.

You will never know what you can do until you do it. Take the risk. Get out of the boat. Jesus made a promise that He would never leave you or forsake you. Take the risk and get out of the boat. The boat being our mind of obstacles thinking that we are not good enough or can't do it. Take the risk and get out of the boat of people. People who say that we can't, never will, and never should.

Take the risk and follow the voice of God!

Face your Fear

Some of the people of God who have been blessed to start a business or even assigned to do so are afraid and will not face their fear. The reality is that the devil knows who you are and what you are going to be in your life. So he has quietly shipped a box of fear to your house and now he's got you.

Take that box and a permeant marker and write on the top of it "Return to sender." According to 2 Timothy 1:7 God has not given you the spirit of fear. So if there is fear in your life it did not come from Christ. It came from the antichrist. The one looking to be more than he is. The father of lies. The deceiver. The truth is you can't trust or believe anything he tells you.

Face your fears. In Joshua 1 God told Joshua that Moses was dead and now it was Joshua's time. During this conversation God told Joshua to be strong and courageous. In fact, in chapter 1 of Joshua the phrase "be strong and courageous" was said nine times. The number 9 symbolizes divine completeness or conveys the meaning of finality.

I believe that God was sharing with Joshua that as long as he was strong and courageous that this divine purpose would be revealed. I also believe that God is saying the same thing to the person who is reading this book right now.

Be strong and courageous and face your fears. The fears that have become obstacles are not from God so be strong and courageous. Seek the face of God daily to get instruction on how you are to navigate these obstacles. Truth be told, Satan will forever try to destroy your authority that you have over him. God gave you dominion and power. So if the devil exercises fear over you, that's because you allowed him to.

Face your fear and know that if God has put it in your path then according to 1 Corinthians 10:13 you also have a way of escape provided by Him. There is nothing you are dealing with that God does not know about. He has allowed certain things in your life to strength you, prepare you, sharpen you.

Like my story above. I ran everywhere that I could when I was by myself. If my grandmother wanted me to go to the store, I ran. During that season of my life we had Walkmans. Okay, I know a large amount of you reading this will never know what that is. With the Walkman I ran and if I did not have it with me, I beat on my chest and sang my song.

Find your rhythm and run your race. You will never know what you can do until you do it. Face your fear.

You have to start somewhere, sometime.

In order for your journey to begin you have to start somewhere sometime. You will never think it is the right time or the right place or you don't have the right money. The Word of God says in Luke 14:28, "Who would think to build a tower and not think of the cost?" Start there!

Yea, yea. I know once you look at the cost of starting this business you will try to position yourself back where you were. But if you will, allow me to speak life into you. I want to tell you something that I had to learn for myself. If God has assigned you to it he will provide for you through it.

Of course, this type of statement has been said so much that it has become a cliché to so many. But it's TRUE! Look back at Joshua for a second and see how God gave him specific directions and if he would follow those directions, he would be successful in the battle he and Israel would have to fight.

One of the first battles was to walk around a wall quietly once a day for six days and then seven times on the seventh day and on the seventh time, shout. What? But because Joshua commanded the Israelites to obey God the wall fell and they were able to conquer it.

Start right where you are and begin to speak to God and ask for direction to what He wants from you. Don't allow the voices of naysayers and doubters to discourage you. If God said it, do it! Proverbs says to trust in the Lord in all your ways. He will direct your path.

As you take the steps to start your Entre-PRAY-neur business, God will order them according to His plan. But you have to start. READY! SET! GO! Find the mentor that God has assigned to you. Find the spiritual leader, the God-guided business leader, and start.

No! I hear you saying, "Well I will start after my kids graduate. I will start once I have a certain amount of money. I will start when God miraculously shows me this is what He wants." NO!

Start. Start by praying, then by planning, then by pacing. The race is not given to the swift but the one who endures until the end. Don't try to be like someone else. Be yourself and go do what God told you to do. You know it is God because you will have a peace about it. You will hear the still small voice and it will give you peace to know that even in the storm God will direct you. Learn to pray in your storm and watch Jesus stand on the edge of your boat and calm your storm. You have to start somewhere sometime.

Why not start now? Of course, there is more to how you do it and in the workbook, I will explain step by step what to do and how to do it. That's why God allowed me to go through the things I did and that's why He allowed others such as Sam Chand, Dr. Robert Watkins, and so many more to be a road marker in my life to push me to this point. The thing that was taught in Dr. Chand's course and leadership forums shaped me to write. The personal encouragement from Dr. Watkins has guided me to jump. The simple text of Dr. Christopher Bowen has strengthened me to go on. The love of my Spiritual Covering Pastor Jeremy Tuck has come alongside to show me the bridges and the potholes. Their help that God has assigned for them to do has helped shape me to a point where I can pen this book and give you what I have.

What I have is not everything, but something that I always say is, "We are as smart or dumb as the people we have around us." Check your circle and start strategizing the shift. Some people will shift out and some people with shift in. Ensure that those you shift in are those sent by God with the help you need.

PRINCIPLE:
Trust the Lord.

APPLICATION:
Walk in faith.

PRAYER:
Lord Jesus, I pray for the man or the woman reading this book right now. I pray that you will help them to always remember what it is that you have already brought them through. Strengthen their faith, Lord Jesus, and constantly remind them that you made a promise that you will never waiver on and that is to be with them at all times. In your name. Amen.

Help Me!
Chapter 5

Joshua 1:14

* Your wives, your little ones, and your livestock shall remain in the land which Moses gave you on this side of the Jordan. <u>But you shall pass before your brethren armed, all your mighty men of valor, and HELP THEM,</u>*

Joshua 1:15

* until the Lord has given your brethren rest, <u>as He gave you,</u> and <u>they also have taken possession of the land which the Lord your God is giving them.</u> Then you shall return to the land of your possession and enjoy it, which Moses the Lord's servant gave you on this side of the Jordan toward the sunrise." (emphasis added)*

I would say in all the years of reading the Scriptures and enjoying many, the Scripture above is one of my favorite chapters. God had set Joshua up to go forward in his next season. In the midst of God giving him direction on what to do in order to move on, God told Joshua nine times to be strong and courageous. But even in strengthening Joshua, the Lord knew he would need some HELP.

God assigned other tribes to the people of Israel to assist them in taking the land that God had already given them. This is not a cliché but real words. If GOD DID IT BEFORE HE WILL DO IT AGAIN! In the last chapter I explained that you must get set and start. I even explained that there is no reason to be afraid as God knows what you need. He knows so well that He has assigned some men and women to assist you in moving forward in the plan structured for your life.

God has blessed so many men and women in their own visions. Why wouldn't God have them to assist you with yours? You and the vision that God has placed in your heart are just as important.

So in the faithfulness of our Lord, He has assigned someone to connect with you in order to either finance your vision, come alongside and partner with you in your vision, or simply pray for your vision. I know as you read the last part, pray for your vision, if you are anything like I was you probably said, "Yes, I need prayer but more importantly I need money to pull this off." I get it, but as an Entre-PRAY-neur, prayer is the foundation of your Christian business. So just as important as the funding for any business, prayer is a constant currency that must go forth to ensure that you don't fail in business.

In the Gospels after Jesus had gone to Golgotha and had proclaimed our forgiveness, He had in fact given His life so that you and I may continue on in our race. There was a man named Joseph, a rich man from Arimathea. During the reading of the Scripture you never heard of him anywhere. His name was never mentioned before this at any time. Yes, it is my opinion that he was near Jesus and maybe even one of His disciples (not one of the twelve). Joseph was assigned to Jesus in one area of His ministry and that was to ensure that Jesus had a gravesite to rest in.

That was it. Joseph showed up and asked for the body of Christ because he purchased a brand-new tomb in order for Jesus' body to be placed in. Imagine that. The same stone we speak about being rolled away is the same stone that Joseph

purchased. It was not about Joseph, a rich man from Arimathea. It was about the fact that it was important for us to see
Jesus go through the worldly ritual of death so that we could
marvel at the spiritual God-directed resurrection.

Who's assigned to you during this season?

So many times in our life lately we have become standoffish,
because you don't know who to trust any more with your life,
your information, your family. In fact, we are not even gathering as families anymore because some don't quite understand
who you are and what the assignment is that God has given
you, so they make vast comments that push you back into your
closet instead of using encouraging words to pull you out.

We have all said, "Forget about it. I will do it myself and
if I can't, then it is okay with me." It is not okay. In fact, the
Bible tells us in many different Scriptures that we are stronger together. The devil wants us to be separated but the Word
of God says let nothing separate what God has put together.
Yes, I hear you. God was talking about marriage. Well if it's
assigned by God to be a communion it is a marriage, merger,
partnership. How many people have made it through terrible
times because of friendships?

So who is God partnering you with that you keep over-
looking because as far as you are concerned that can't be the
right connection? Surely God is not asking you to partner in
business with the very person on your job that gets on your
last nerve. The Lord just cannot be asking you to go into your
CEO's office, even though somehow God has caused you to
be pretty close, to ask for an investment into your company.
Your creator couldn't possibly want you to ask your in-laws to
support your dream. WHY NOT?

This is why we are called Entre-PRAY-neurs. Because in all things we seek the face of God to direct us. If God has assigned you to that person or those persons then He has already placed on the hearts of whomever it is to bless you. That's the thing about the creator. He knows exactly what you need. You're saying, "Okay, but what if they say no and this person is who I heard God say to go to?" Well you keep praying. Everyone in your life is not all there for the same season. Some are not approved for this season but are for either one coming up or one that has passed.

We must continue to seek the face of God for direction and timing. Remember they are probably just like you at this point in their life of hearing what God wants: skeptical. I mean if they have been assigned to you to give you millions of dollars and they have up to this point been great stewards of what God entrusted them with, why would they not be? I pray that they are in prayer with God as well to ensure that you are the right person and ready yourself.

Each of us has preparation time for the next level. You might be great now with money but having a hard time with leadership. So because of that if you started now and had the money you would not have the right team, because people don't leave bad jobs, they leave bad bosses. So if you are not a good leader, in fact a great leader, you could destroy what God is planning.

Leadership

It is my opinion that there are some natural born leaders, but I also believe that everyone can be a leader if they have the proper training, by the proper trainer. Who are you following? Who is the person or persons that you are allowing to lead you in words and deeds? I am a true believer that you are as good, bad, or great as those who are around you. If you want to know what kind of person you are, look at the people you spend the majority of your time with.

Whomever you are most around is the one who is leading you. Now research and study their character and habits. What are they teaching you directly or indirectly? What kind of heart do they have? Do they have a God heart or a dark heart? Motivational speaker Jim Rohn made a statement that I have read and heard multiple times from others as well. I am not sure who coined it, but it makes since to me. He stated that we are the average of the five people we spend the most time with. This relates to the law of averages, which is the theory that the result of any given situation will be the average of all outcomes.

Over the years I have read books by John Maxwell, Sam Chand, T.D. Jakes, and many more on leadership and leadership is a topic of major conversation. If you want to make it far in the business that you are in, you don't want to get a mentor who knows nothing about what you are doing. Don't misunderstand me. I have a couple of mentors and not all of them know business or know ministry or know real estate, but I have one or two for each area of my life.

I have just acquired a mentor for a new journey in my life of writing books, songs, and transitioning into other business ventures that God has instructed me to move forward in. In fact, a couple of them are in the courting stage as I want to ensure that this is what God has for me in this season and that they are the leaders I need leading me in this season.

Who is leading you? And where are they leading you?

I am sorry if you have never been down this road before either in success or failure. Yes, I said in failure. See their assignment may simply be to show me what not to do. There may be another in my life who has the intellect to show me what to do. My focus at this point is to hear what God is saying and do what God is telling me. I don't have all the knowledge that's why I have mentors, but I do have enough where I can turn around and serve the next person whom God may assign me to assist.

Turn Around and Serve

God gives seed to the sower. The Word of God states that God will not put more on you then you can bear (1 Corinthians 10:13). I am a true believer that the thing that you and I have to bear is in order to share our testimony with those that God knew would not be strong enough to handle themselves. God sees you as honorable enough to allow you to endure the test so that you can share your experience with the one you will mentor.

Turn around and serve. So often in my life have I known that a person had the knowledge to assist another but failed to do so because they didn't want to see that person thrive. Crabs in a barrel they say. I would simply say they are selfish. That's it. There are enough businesses, money, and people out here for all of us. You are assigned to some and so am I. We must learn to share.

The whole idea of doing business God's way is so that we can take the gospel to the masses. Jesus Christ instructed us before He ascended into Heaven to go make disciples, baptize them, and most importantly teach them to obey all that He had commanded. We can't do that if we never turn around and serve. The knowledge that you have should be shared with the next generation.

While I was managing multiple family housing as well as while I served in the military, I learned to replace myself. I know it seems crazy to work myself out of a job, but if I do it right, I can work myself up the ladder. So, I replace myself. I train the people I lead in a way that when I leave, I can give a strong recommendation of who should be next in the seat.

Why would I do that? Well then I don't have to go and interview thousands of people who will lie on a resume and in your face, then they come in and they are nothing like what they said they are. The one, however, that I have prepared to take my place is already ready and if I am moving up then they are still part of my team. So, I'm still winning.

You only open a business to sell or will. Sometimes the person you will the business to is not family. Not every person is created to do what you do, so you have to find that person that God has assigned to take your place. Even in the sell I know it is about the money in a business sell, but you should be so God focused that you have even sought the face of the Lord on who to sell to.

The person to take your business name that you built on the principles of God should not be able to come in with a dark heart or deceitful mind and handle God's great people. So, the best way to handle that is to turn around and serve. Yes, what once was your baby is now going to be someone else's, but you are not concerned because you have turned around and served in such a way that you know exactly whose hands it is in.

There are young men and women who would thrive from the leadership of a great person such as yourself. Turn around and serve them, because they will be the next politician, businessman or woman, seed sower, and much more. Wouldn't it be better to be kind to them, doing it God's way?

PRINCIPLE:
Evaluate your surroundings.

APPLICATION:
Have some one-on-one lunches to see who is for you and who is not.

PRAYER:
Lord Jesus, I pray for the man or the woman reading this book right now. I pray that you will open their eyes and allow them to see that there are more of us in the Kingdom of God who are for them than those in the world against them. Assist them in recognizing who you have assigned to help them accomplish this mission and be successful as an Entre-PRAY-neur. In your name. Amen.

Embrace the Failures
Chapter 6

Romans 8:1, 2

¹ There is therefore now no condemnation to those who are in Christ Jesus, who do not walk according to the flesh, but according to the Spirit. ² For the law of the Spirit of life in Christ Jesus has made me free from the law of sin and death.

1 Corinthians 10:13

¹³ No temptation has overtaken you except such as is common to man; but God is faithful, who will not allow you to be tempted beyond what you are able, but with the temptation will also make the way of escape, that you may be able to bear it.

Failures are the womb of success

In 2007 when I first started my journey in Bible college I had no idea what I would have to endure as it relates to the failures and the triumph that I would face as well. Isn't that the worst thing you can deal with, the unknown? I spent a lot of time in the military traveling and what it took to accomplish things there, but had absolutely no idea of what it would take for me to first finish something that I started.

At that point in life I hadn't finished anything that I started. I was expelled from every high school that I went to. I had to go to technical school to get into the military because I did not have a high school diploma. Now that I was registering to start a new journey at school the failures of my past were chasing me down. Yes at first everything was okay. It was explained to me that I could use my military DD214 in order to register for classes and I would not need a high school diploma, because the DD214 was accepted in its place.

Needless to say, approximately halfway through my course study at Beulah Heights University I received a call the week before the next semester was to start. The voice on the other end of the call was sympathetic but factual. "Mr. Broomfield, this is _____. It has come to our attention that we do not have your diploma on file. Please bring that to us at soon as you can or you will not be able to continue on with this course."

My response was, "Well I guess I will withdraw." The voice on the other end exclaimed, "Why?!" This particular person was previously a professor that I was honored to be instructed by. She said to me, "Vincent, come on what's going on?" So I confessed that as a young man I did not take high school serious and so I did not finish high school. Of course there are questions in your mind because by now she has information about me such as the fact that I spent approximately 15 years serving in the military. So she asked, "Well how is that possible?" Again I stated that my mindset in high school was not one of academics.

So being the person that she is she encouraged me to go and take the GED course and get my high school equivalence. I thought, No! I am not going to embarrass myself by taking a test that I know I will fail. At this junction in my life, that's how I felt. Like a pure failure, a whole failure, and no one could really tell me differently. She went on to try and convince me until we simply ended the call. During this point in my life I had owned a few businesses. I had just finished eight and a half years active duty, and six years reserve. I obtained my realtors license in 1999 and made good money doing it.

The accomplishments however could not change my mind on how much of a failure I felt like. I went home to a wonderful lady who is now my wife and I told her jokingly what happened and how I would not be able to finish, again, what I started. She began to ask, "Well why can't you go and get your GED?" Okay, not this again. I'm just not going to do it. I'm sure what I said was something similar to that, because I know where I was mentally in life at that point.

I was divorced, a school drop-out, didn't finish anything that I started and here I go again. So later the next evening when Zenobia got home she came in the house with this huge GED study guide and I said to her, "No! Not going to do it!" I left that book right there all week. I had convinced myself that I was a complete failure and it was just no sense to go through the process all over. On Friday of that week Zenobia said to me, "Okay, you need to go to sleep so you can be restful for your test taking tomorrow in Macon, Georgia."

Anger, questions, doubt, fear, all that stuff that went through my mind at the time. I was not ready to do this. Then of course she told me that she had already paid for the testing. Okay now you know I do not like losing money. So I went to take the test for five to six hours and drive back home. A couple weeks later I went to get the results at the main office in Decatur, Georgia and WOW! I passed with flying colors. Of course I went to the school immediately to share the news and register for the next semester before it was too late.

During this time of registration there was a book that had been given to us that was written by Dr. Sam Chand. Failure: The Womb of Success. As I read the testimonies of so many people, this book blessed my soul. *I can do this,* I said to myself. It's not how you start but how you finish. In my prayer time I could hear the word experiences, experiences. What did it mean? I prayed and asked God for direction.

Experiences Exposed

As I began to reflect on the hand of God in my life and then hear His voice as it relates to the word experiences, I hear exposed. I am confused of course now and want clarity on what these two words I keep hearing mean. Then one day as I was preparing a paper for one of the professors, as I reread what was written I could see that the experiences God allowed me to go through, the experiences that God has now exposed to me are the very experiences that He did, is, and will use to continue to bless me.

When you apply for a job they want you to send them your resume. The very thing that you map out all or most of your experiences on to prove that you are worthy of being inter-viewed for the job. I have been on both sides of that table a large part of my life. Managing multi-family housing for years I was able to review and pick through resumes that painted the picture for me of the candidates who were going out for the position. In fact, I have sent my resume many times to get included in the race for employment.

As you take a look at your resume and see the very things that you have done for years for other people I want you to ask and answer why can't you do those things for yourself? In order for a resume to be what it is, a person has to go through the fire of trials. Now that fire may mean a large amount of failures. Maybe you were fired at one point in your life. Maybe you were released because of a personal issue. None of that can change your resume.

As you look at your experiences exposed you should begin to realize that God has allowed others to train you on what would make you. Let's look at David for a second. In 1 Samuel 17, David told Saul that he had experience protecting the sheep and fighting off lions and bears. So when it was time to fight off Goliath, David was prepared and confident. At that juncture of life, he had worked out the kinks. If you have been on your job doing the same thing for at least five years or more, you have experience equivalent to a bachelors' degree.

This is the reason a large amount of companies accept a bachelors' degree or work experience. Don't discount what you have endured in life. God is going to use those pains and heartaches to bless you. The problems that you had in life are the very things that will propel you to your purpose in the kingdom. My wife and I often say her mantle and my mantle are different. In other words, don't compare yourself to the next person and what they have or what they are doing. Your mantle is your mantle. Learn how to take your exposed experiences and turn them into a God-driven business.

Remember God doesn't allow you to go through anything that He will not use at a later time to bless you. I said it before and will continue to say it. Proverbs tells us that our talents are going to make room for us. They will put us in front of people that you and I would absolutely not believe we are in front of. You may feel that in this part of your life you can't do it, but I am here to tell you that it will not be you who does it but God through you. The experiences that you have had in life are going to expose who you really are.

Yes, there have been some failures in life that have embarrassed you, lowered your self-esteem, and maybe even brought on depression. You are a better person for it. I personally don't want anyone teaching, leading, or guiding me who has never failed. Failure should be part of your foundation.

Failures Foundation

In the book that Dr. Chand wrote about failures he highlighted the life and failures of a large amount of people. In the descriptions of each person Dr. Chand exposed some of the failures of the people but then shared how they were the foundation to their success. Your failures in life are as well part of your foundation. They have assisted you in what to do and what not to do. Your failures have built the guardrails of your life. In marriage, business, parenting, employment you have been building your resume out of your failures.

It is because you failed that test in college that you now have developed a greater study habit. It's because you were fired that you changed your work ethics. It is because of that unfortunate divorce that you learned how to be a better husband or wife. It is because of experiencing the failure of that run-down car that you take care of the one you have so well. That stint of time you were home unemployed, power off, peeping out of the window to see if they were coming to get your car that you have taken the financial class and become a great finance expert.

These areas of your life that you have failed in will be some of the areas that you will begin to write books about, you will open your financial literacy program. It is because of those things that you will find yourself not being invited to the table of others but being asked if they can come to yours. Jesus taught that it is not wise to build a house on sand, because when the storm comes through the house will fall. Whereas when you build the house on a rock it will last the winds and the weight of the storms.

You are built on the rock of Jesus Christ who has empowered you to stand through your failures. You are stronger because of it. You are wiser because of it. You will be able to do this business in God's name because you have failures that have exposed your experiences and become the foundation to your success.

PRINCIPLE:
Downs come with the ups.

APPLICATION:
Turn your mistakes in to learning experiences and then use them to make a difference.

PRAYER:
Lord Jesus, I pray for the man or the woman reading this book right now. I pray that you encourage them in your Word that they are not a failure but an intelligent being who you have created to be and do more. Remove all low self-esteem Lord and help them to see that the experiences were put there for a reason. It in your name that we pray. Amen.

Against All Odds
Chapter 7

Philippians 4:13 (NLT)
13 For I can do everything through Christ,[a] who gives me strength.

Romans 8:37 (NLT)
37 No, despite all these things, overwhelming victory is ours through Christ, who loved us.

I mentioned Joshua the servant of Moses in a previous chapter and so I want to stay in the vein of his victory by sharing his testimony. In Numbers chapter 13 there is a dialogue of sending spies to the land of Canaan to see what God had already given the children of Israel even if they had not as of that moment acquired it. The spies left as one and came back divided on what they in the flesh would be able to do. Across the Jordan in the Land of Canaan there were giants and fruit in abundance. More than they had ever seen before and even imagined.

Twelve spies went over and saw the greatest of the land, but because of the mental state of some versus the others when they returned ten of the twelve declared that they could not conquer the land because they were like grasshoppers to the giants. Two of the spies (Joshua and Caleb) thought completely different as it related to the conquering of the land. I believe Joshua was on the optimistic side of things because he was the servant to Moses and therefore was on the in of what he heard God say and what he saw God do. Joshua knew that this was not going to be a task for the God he served.

The other ones on the other hand did not have that grace. Their fear caused them to believe in their hearts and walk in discouragement of being able to conquer the land. This ladies and gentlemen is where a large amount of men and women of faith live. They suffer with the ten who said they could not. God has called us to be the head and not the tail. So why is it that we are living beneath our call?

We have the disease of doubt. See in the narrative the ten declared loudly that the Israelites were not able to conquer that land because of the slave mentality that continued to flood their minds. It is my total belief that the mind that we have will be the life that we live. During a family meeting the ten said we cannot but Joshua said that we can. It was a family dispute and the ten won. In fact the influence the man of God Moses to go with them which caused him as well not to enter into the promise land.

Joshua on the other hand after years had passed was promoted and charged with conquering the land. This again is where a large amount of people are when it comes to the generational curses in our lives. Because the grandparent and parents said we can't, we don't. But we have to understand the mindset of that culture. See slavery had not been too far dispersed when those who were born in the 70s still heard we can't.

When God called Joshua and told him to gather the children of Israel and go conquer the land, there was no doubt in the mind of Joshua. The Lord told him to be strong and courageous over nine times for a reason. Joshua was made aware that this was not going to be a cake walk but it would happen. I want to encourage you. This is not going to be a cake walk but it will happen. Keep your hand in God's hand, entre-PRAY-neur. It will all work out. Against all odds you will succeed in your business and it will generate generational wealth and knowledge.

Needless to say the ten and all of the old generation of the Israelites did not see the promised land let alone conquer it. Joshua, however was able to stay faithful and against all odds pull it off. Let me put a pin here and explain to you that doubt is the anchor to faith. Your dream can float and soar as long as you keep doubt away from it. As soon as doubt comes on board it anchors the ship of your dream.

You Can Do This

As one of our chapter Scriptures depicts, you can do all things through Christ who strengthens you. Yes, I know that in your strength you may feel a certain way on how this will happen or not happen. I am here to tell you that you were built for this and in God's plan you are victorious. You can do this. Follow the plan of visions and you will soar.

See this was the testimony of Joshua. He, after the family dispute, kept the faith and even when God called him he walked it out. He took charge of his destiny and moved forward. He lead as a kingdom leader does and so will you. You can do this, with the help of the Holy Spirit. You can do this.

Whenever I think about how hard things get sometimes and in that same moment battle the words of doubt. As you read I said battle the words of doubt not fall victim to them. I am constantly reminded about how Peter took on the risk and got out of the boat. Against all odds, naysayers, and doubt, Peter stepped out on faith. The word of God says that you will never be tempted beyond what you can handle. You can do this.

It every situation God has not only prepared for you strength to deal with the obstacle but he also prepared for you a way of escape. So get out of the home of depression and go forward. Get up off your bed of affliction and move forward. You got this! You have been working this hobby for years and now God is about to monetize it for you and cause your family for generations to be wealthy. It starts with you.

Get out of the boat and move forward in faith. Move forward in strength, move forward in wisdom. God has prepared you for this. Remember Jeremiah 29:11, God says I know the PLANS that I have for you. Plans to prosper you and give you hope. Go forth and prosper in your gift.

It is now time for your name to be known. What if James would have been the one to take the risk and get out of the boat? We would not be talking about Peter. We would be shouting about James. JAMES GOT OUT OF THE BOAT AND WALKED ON WATER! Well because you are going to start the business in the name of the Lord your name will be made known.

Let me dispense the doubt and excuses.

WHY NOT YOU?

So often as a pastor I meet people that I try and encourage and their excuses are greater than their talents. If you could sell excuses the world would be rich. After letting the majority of them finish with their excuses, not all of them make it before I cut them off, I ask them the questions, "Why not you? Why can't you do what Steve Jobs did? Why can't you invent the next chef robot? Why can't you perfect the self-driving car? Why not you?"

What makes you any different from the CEO of a big corporation? Of course there is the hustle, the grind, the work ethic, but in creation and vision there's no difference. You have a dream like Steve Jobs, like Warren Buffet, why not you? My belief of why not is the fact that you are not surrounded as of yet with the right people to encourage you and get behind your vision. See you are as good (or not) as the people you have around you.

Who is the supporter around you? Who is the marketer that will market your dream? Who is the branding specialist? Who is the money person? See you can do this, but you must, however find the people that God has assigned to be by your side.

You also must control your expectations and patience. In other words, set the expectation that your business will do well but know that it will happen in God's timing. Remember when Mary and Martha became upset with Jesus and told Him that had He been there on time Lazarus would not have died? Well Jesus asked them, "Didn't I tell you that this was not unto death but onto the Glory of God?"

Don't become impatient with the movement of your vision. Just ensure that you stay constant in prayer to seek the guidance of the Holy Spirit and the direction of God. He has your front, back, from side to side. The vision came from Him therefore it is His responsibility to fund it, grow it. Yes, you are his hands and feet so you must always have an ear to hear what your next move is. But as long as you do the things that God commands you to do, why not you?

You have to go out now and conquer. Romans chapter eight tells us that we are not just conquerors but we are more than conquerors.

Go Conquer

That means that we don't just create, we multiply things that will bless this world. We take note of the things of this world that can be better or that the world needs to be introduced to and we are the ones to do it. Go forth and conquer. The talent that God has embedded into your heart and being will be the very thing that the world will need at the time that they need it. Yes, I get it you may not see how it is going to get done, but just know that with God on your side it will happen.

Now go overcome and take control of the world in your field of experience. Go conquer the sports world. Brand yourself as a Christian and know that yes, the world will try to block your blessings but your prayers are stronger than their block. Go forward and conquer the car industry and develop something greater than what we have. To be more than a conquer we go beyond what we see and what the world says we can do. The film industry will never be the same now that Mr. Tyler Perry has come in and created his own.

Psalm 23 says that God will prepare a table for you in the presence of your enemies. This is not to boast in you but to boast in testimony that the wall of Jericho will come down with a simple unified shout. There is absolutely nothing you can't do as long as you have God on your side. The 3D printer was created by Chuck Hall in the mid 1980s. It did not instantly take off but now is being used all over the world to print architect designs for corporations to get a full view of what their next building will look like. The printer is used by car manufacturers to see what the new designed car will physically look like.

I am simply saying this the world is waiting for you to conquer. The world is awaiting that thing, business, book, car, home that you will create and introduce to the world. Go forward and conquer.

PRINCIPLE:
Never give up.

APPLICATION:
Go forth and conquer that which God has put in your hand and path.

PRAYER:
Lord Jesus, I pray for the man or the woman reading this book right now. I pray that you light a fire on the inside of them and help them to be strong and courageous. Help them to know that you would have never given it to them if you were not confident that they could handle it. In your name. Amen.

Give to Get
Chapter 8

2 Corinthians 9:6(NKJV)

⁶ But this I say: He who sows sparingly will also reap sparingly, and he who sows bountifully will also reap bountifully.

2 Corinthians 9:10(NLT)

¹⁰ For God is the one who provides seed for the farmer and then bread to eat. In the same way, he will provide and increase your resources and then produce a great harvest of generosity in you.

Well we absolutely can't say that we are in ministry or about God's business and not want to live by this principle. This is one of the main principles of any house, ministry, Christian, or business. If we want to be literal, you have to give to get. The principle of Second Corinthians is plain and to the point. How you give is how you will receive. This principle, however, is one of the main principles that stunts the growth of any Christian-based, Jesus-proclaimed ministry. Your business will be or is a ministry that God will use to bless His great people.

Giving is a part of ministry. Giving is what Jesus did for all who accept Him. He gave, so that you and I could do that very same thing. In fact Jesus spoke a statement that speaks to our doing. He said that the thing that He did we would do greater. Jesus fed, Jesus healed, Jesus brought back to life, Jesus ensured that He put the business of God first and then Himself second. This is the mentality that you must encumber when it comes to doing business God's way.

Matthew speaks to putting first the kingdom of God and all of His righteousness and all these other things would be added unto you. The other things are the things that you seek in your life. The other things are the things that Psalms speak of which are the desires of your heart. The things such as your business flourishing, such as your family being in unity and not division, things such as your relationship being loving and fruitful. I must admonish you to focus on the kingdom of God and not the things, but understand that this is a principle that comes with a promise. A promise from God no less, rather than a promise from a friend, family, or investor. When you operate your business in such a way that God is first and foremost, then that business begins and continues to soar.

For a few years I was blessed to work at the main campus of Chick-fil-A. During this time of employment, it was mind blowing to realize that the chicken is the fuel to do all of the other God business that the company is focused on. One of the things or moments that I enjoyed about the company and time that I was there is when I went in to the front door. Right at the front door there is a monument that reads the company's mission statement. The company's mission statement is "To glorify God by being a faithful steward of all that is entrusted to us. To have a positive influence on all who come in contact with Chick-fil-A."

They absolutely make an influential impact on those in the community and on the job. They do this by giving. The company main office included (not sure if the setup is the same) multiple foundations, missions department, and of course all of the departments that carry the vision and mission. I would have to say that from what I observed in their caring for the staff and customers, that CFA (Chick-fil-A) has a mindset of harvest.

A Mindset of Harvest

What exactly is a mindset of harvest? Glad you asked. This is the mind that is focused on the seeds that are sown. Understanding the farming industry and simple common sense is to say that you understand the more seeds that you sow equates to the harvest that you will reap. In fact in the typical seed sowing, when you plant one seed you do not just get one seed returned to you. The plant that is derived from this seed typically brings forth a product that multiplies that very seed in its produce.

Take for instance the tomato seed that is small in size. This seed once planted will in time produce a vine of tomatoes that as well has seeds of multiplicity in it. The tomato has seeds in it and the vine has multiple tomatoes on it. So one seed produces and has the possibility to produce double, triple, even a hundred fold of what is its size. So with this narrative in mind we see that to plant a seed is to know that in time there will be a harvest of plentiful. This is the mind of harvest.

A farmer doesn't go through the process of tilling the ground and setting up a watering system in order to just plant one seed. That would have his business in the red instead of the black. In Genesis chapter one, God gave us a command to be fruitful and multiply. The reason you enter into business is to step out of the boat and multiply your intellectual property, your great talent, or the secret recipe that your grandmother left you that everyone who comes into contact with it loves.

You know that once you properly master the task of dupli-cating the recipe that it will heighten the taste buds of so many that now you can monetize it and multiply it to so many who will pay absolutely what it is worth. Where your grandmother was simply trying to feed her family you now have the mind-set to establish your family name through one recipe (seed).

It is the mindset that propels us or stops us from doing that which God has preplanned. Go preplanned for the Israelites to conquer the land and in His words stated for them to go and spy what He had already given them. It was the mindset that stopped them from achieving the harvest. Romans again tells us that the mind set on the flesh receives the things of the flesh and that is death, but the mind set on the spirit (kingdom of God) receives the things of the spirit which are life. (Romans 8; emphasis included)

To go further with this encouragement to think yourself free from a nine to five, free from the bill collectors calling and knocking on your door, financially free if properly done is to say what Proverbs says, "For as he thinks in his heart, so is he. To effectively pull this business off God's way you must think like God. I mean you were made in His image and likeness.

The Law of Reciprocity

Giving falls under the Law of reciprocity. Whatever you give out will return to you in a form of multiples. It's the very law that is spoken of in Second Corinthians 9:6. If you give a small amount you will receive a small amount. If you give in a major way (bountifully), however you will get back in a major way. This year you have put a lot of stuff into your life. You have allowed other people to put stuff in your life. You tolerated some things being planted in your life. The Law of

Reciprocity says that whatever you put in is what you will get out.

If all you put in your body is sugar, unhealthy foods, alcohol, drugs, salt, and everything else, when you go to the doctor and they draw blood you will see all of the effects of the salt, drugs, alcohol, and everything else. If you planted seeds in your life then harvest is seeking you, because of the Law of Reciprocity. If you planted apple seeds you can expect an apple tree. If you plant orange seeds you can expect an orange tree. I hope that I am blessing some entre-PRAY-neur's heart today. The joy is in the planting of the seed because of the fact that you know when you plant the seed you are now living in the season of expectation. Because it's a Law that what you put in is what you will get out. First Corinthians 3:5-9 declares that one plants, one waters, but God gives the increase!

I want to declare to my entre-PRAY-neur that God is calling forth the harvest of increase in your life. You have chosen to plant your seed instead of eating your seed. Understanding that it may seem harmless to eat and swallow an apple seed thinking it would be okay. One seed will not hurt but after time of eating the seed over and over again will cause sickness over your life. Let me explain. The apple seed has a protective covering that breaks down effectively when it is planted. This however is not effective when it is eaten. The ingredients of the seed were designed to produce the nutrients of what the seed needs to grow into a harvest. But those same ingredients will kill you if you chew on them. The apple seed has cyanide in it and cyanide is a poison that will kill you if you intake it. All that said, don't eat your seed. Eating your seed will KILL you!

I expect that each entre-PRAY-neur has planted seed all year. Seed of greatness, love, monetary funds, forgiveness, peace. If you have planted those seeds, then I want to let you know that you can expect a harvest of peace in your life in this season. You can expect a harvest new business coming to you in this season. You can expect a FINANCIAL harvest in your life. The Law of Reciprocity declares what you put in is what you are going to get out. Some of you may be shouting right now because you know what you have planted. I want to encourage you to SHOUT like you have lost your mind. SHOUT! SHOUT! SHOUT! The harvest is here.

God Gives Seed to the Sower

The harvest is here because God gives seed to the sower. He gave you seed because He knew that you have practiced for years on how to be a great steward over what He has given you. He trusts you just like you trust Him. God knew that once He tried you and tested you over and over again, He would finally make a vessel pleasing on to Him. Now that you have become that vessel God looks into your life and sees a sower. To give you seed is to care for His children in so many ways with you.

Your harvest has begun to spring up in your life, in your business, and family. You have been wondering, not worrying, how this business transaction would be complete. With what funds were you going to fund your business opportunity? How in the world are you going to be able to operate a smooth transition from one full-time job to a full-time business? God will provide all the time, energy, partners, friends, and much more that you need.

It is going to work because God has looked into your heart and found your heart to have the same rhythm as His. You think like He does. The image that God sees now compared to years ago is more like the image of His soon. Now instead of you losing sleep at night wondering how exactly are you going to structure this business financially and in man power, you fall to sleep in faith knowing that God has you covered.

To say that God gives seed to the sower is to say that He will provide all your needs. The start-up funds, I prophesy, God has planned for you. Investors are coming from every side of life. As an entre-PRAY-neur you will pray on each investment offer in order to weed out the angels from the devils. God is showing you even now who He has provided for in order for them to provide for you.

The funds to hire the business consultant, like myself or many others, will be supplied. The names of trustworthy Christian attorneys that have applied the same principles of God's Word are at your fingertips. All of you are praying and God is directing your runway to who is cleared to land in your new season of life and who is not. Live the principle of prayer and planning. God is about to rock your world.

Your harvest is big because your prayers have been big. Your business will be huge because your worship has been huge. The people that you will touch and change are the ministry of your business. Jesus left you a great commission, not just for your immediate life, but for every aspect of your life. Your business is now the new avenue to reach the people of God.

PRINCIPLE:
Giving is the principle.

APPLICATION:
Always seed into what you want God to do for you.

PRAYER:

Lord Jesus, I pray for the man or the woman reading this book right now. I pray that you water every seed that you have placed in their hands to plant. Guide them as it relates to where to plant the seed. Then Lord I pray that their harvest will be more than expected. In your name. Amen.

More Than One
Chapter 9

Ecclesiastes 11:1, 2 (NLT)

¹ Send your grain across the seas, and in time, profits will flow back to you. ² But divide your investments among many places, for you do not know what risks might lie ahead.

Genesis 1:28 (NLT)

²⁸ Then God blessed them and said, "Be fruitful and multiply. Fill the earth and govern it. Reign over the fish in the sea, the birds in the sky, and all the animals that scurry along the ground."

As the Scripture reads in Ecclesiastes 11:2, "divide your investments among many places, for you do not know what risk might lie ahead." In other words, in fact my words, have seven or yes, eight streams of income so that when the earth has famine you do not feel it. In my youth, this was explained to me by my grandmother saying, "Baby, don't put all your eggs in one basket." By putting them in one basket you run the risk of dropping that basket and all your eggs breaking. If you, however, spread them over seven or eight baskets, you still have risk but it lowers the chance of losing everything.

Over the years I have struggled with what this means and how to properly exercise this, but through failure and trials I have figured it out. When I was younger I had my hands in everything. Well even now I do as well, but cutting back on what my hands are on and focusing on what can work is hard for me. I'll explain later in the chapter. But I would have a job here and side hustle there. I can install TVs and car radios. I can work on computers and bake you a cake. I can repair a car, and build you a table. People in my life would often call me a Jack of all trades, master of none. I absolutely hated that. The last part would always get me and even now it bites a little. A master of NONE.

I tried for years to shut my brain off from saying oh I can do that or letting the dreadful words come out of my mouth loud enough for someone to hear me. Once they heard me people always need something done. So they would say can you do this or that? Please don't misunderstand me. The majority of what I did I charged for. As a young man or even now as an adult, by using the skill God gave me, He is providing for me.

See the phrase Jack of all trades master of none, or being categorized a Jamaican doesn't bother me as much because I know that behind this act of skill comes a profit of some kind. So this essentially means I always have money in my pocket. If something came up and I needed some quick cash legally by the way, I could make someone a logo, or design a post card. I could install a quick radio in their car. I could repair a computer or iPhone screen. Quickly I would have a couple hundred dollars in my pocket.

Earlier I said I would explain that I am trying to cut back on what my hands are doing. I simply mean I am strategically transitioning from such hard work with less turn around profit to a more thought-type work with more profit. See you get paid more for your intellectual property. So the plan to retire and leave something major for my kids comes with what I call horizontal money. The money you make while you are sleep. Yes there are multiple ways you can make money while you are asleep. Real estate investments, song writing, book writing, stock (if you know what you're doing), and so many others.

Once you have effectively learned how to achieve this method or operate in this principle then you have effectively learned how to live off of streams.

Streams of Income

Streams of income simply means that you have multiple streams or revenues of income coming into your bank account or bank accounts. Imagine this in the book of Genesis. God put Adam in the Garden that had multiple streams feeding it. The plants, trees, and anything else that would profit from a stream of water could live off of them. If one dried up there were a couple more to ensure that needs were met.

This is what streams of income means. Let me cancel the thought of seven to eight full-time jobs. No that would put you in the grave a lot sooner than you want to be. Maybe even sooner than God wants you there. The seven to eight streams are smart streams. For instance, let's say you work a full-time job and as you have been there for years you have bought into the job's 401k (stocks). You have purchased and moved to three different homes, but instead of selling each one you kept them to become a landlord. After a while you learned how to operate in tax lien properties and now you have multiple properties bring in an income each.

You have prayed and followed the voice of God to invest in a friend's business that has taken off and now that is a stream of income. You decided to take the knowledge you have acquired over the years and put it in a book and it sells. You love getting up on Saturdays cutting lawns and now you have a portfolio of five lawns paying a minimum of forty bucks each, every week. That is an $800 to $1,000 stream per month, or $12,000 for the year. Just in the small thought process of multiple streams you have six incomes coming into your home just from you. If you are married then now there are maybe a couple more coming from your spouse. You give a tenth at the least to church, entre-PRAY-neur, and you ensure to put a tenth away in a saving account and now you have financial freedom.

Multiple streams of smart income will allow you to live way below your means and have a pretty nice life. This is what God wants for each of His great people. Everyone does not and may not ever get it, but you do and now you can teach your offspring by way of what they see and what you sit down and teach them. You have written the prescription for your family and bloodline to be financially wealthy. This is what God meant in His Scripture when He had it written for us to be the head and not the tail, above and not beneath, lender and not borrower.

So many have made these statements that they have become cliché and lost the true value of what God intended for them to be. He literally wants you to have enough streams that now you can open a bank and become a lender to mortgage companies. You and your family have become such great stewards that now everyone has a healthy bank account(s) and this represents being above and not beneath (well off versus living paycheck to paycheck). When you walk into car dealerships or electronic stores you can demand the price of something because you have the check book to pay for it instantly and the representative of that dealership or store sees you as the head and not the tail.

Do the streams of income paint a different perspective to you yet? This is what God meant by be fruitful and multiply. Of course I know you thought it meant having sex and making babies. In reality, the Scripture is that God wants us to be fruitful (income) and multiply it (streams). This principle is missed by so many in life and they find themselves in the everyday rat race that when they retire and there has been a famine in the land or the 401k that they have leaned on to be there had to be used for kids' medical bills, now they have to work a second and third job to keep up the lifestyle they once had.

Yes, you do need a focused specialty. The main job that will be the rock foundation to what feeds your family, but streams of income from smart sources is biblical.

Focused Specialty

There absolutely has to be a focused specialty. I have come to learn that you can have streams of income from one focused specialty without losing your mind on so many different thoughts of making money and providing for your home. Take your specialty and make multiple stream from it, which means the only thing you have to become great at is balancing your time. Okay, let's get a little more understanding of what this looks like.

Let's take the accountant. The accountant works for a company that pays them to balance the debts and credits for eight hours a day. Then there is a small mom and pop shop that just opened and they need help setting up and balancing books. While you are teaching them to do this you get permission from them to video it and post it in a YouTube channel that now has a large following, because who knew there would be thousands of people out in the world who want to know how to set up and balance books? Because of the large following, YouTube begins to send you checks from the advertising they sold and promoted on your page. The accountant has become so requested that now they have a focus group helping them strategize how to monetize this focused specialty.

The book titled "You Are an Accountant" is set to be released now because you have so many requests that you can't be everywhere at the same time. (This is not a real book by the way, at least not until you write it.) With your book comes an online masterclass that people are signing up for and seminars to follow. All reasonably priced so even the beginner can achieve new knowledge. The accountant's focused specialty now has at a minimum of six streams of income without having to do way more than necessary.

If you have worked in a position or practiced a skill for more than three to five years, you have become a professional. You can have multiple streams that come from that focused specialty. You do not have to put on so many different hats that you lose your hair. Look right in the mirror and see what God has blessed you with and focus on that. Pray that God will open your eyes and give you a narrow focus for what is right in your hand. When I say narrow focus, I don't mean small. I mean tunneled to that one skill in many ways.

What's in your hand? What gifts has God given you that He has planned for you to use to sustain your life? How can you turn this focused specialty into a multiple stream income? How can you change the trajectory of your life? What you focus on is what you will become great at. If you focus on the pity party then you will become great at that. If you focus on the excuses then you will become great at that. If you look inside of you to find what it is God put there that is the thing that God wants to bless you with and turn your midnight into day.

What I don't want you to do however is try to be something you are not. The Jack of all trades master of none can harm you. You will always be trying to find that get rich quick scheme that you will lose your mind, possibly your family, and your way. I want to encourage you, don't do it. Focus on what you are great at and the good stuff leave for fun.

Don't Do it!

For many that do not know exactly what it is they are good at they will begin to try their hand at everything. Don't do it! In every business, relationship, job, ministry, whatever it is, it takes three to five years for it to begin to produce for you. If you keep jumping from one task or the next best thing you will never allow that one thing, that focused specialty, to shine in your life.

Don't get caught up in what someone else is doing that they make look so easy. It is not always easy. It may be for them because it is their focused specialty. For you it would be a struggle because you don't know how to wear it. Let's look at David and Saul. When David was preparing to fight Goliath Saul put his own armor on David. Now according to Scripture Saul was the largest of the Israelites. Saul was a warrior in size. David was a shepherd in size but a warrior in heart. The armor that Saul put on David was too big and its weight was built for Saul to handle not David.

David's focused Specialty was a slingshot and a stone. He picked up five stones but he only needed to handle one at a time. The other four were for Goliath's brothers. David said to Saul, "I cannot wear these for I have not tested them." Be as smart and wise as David when it comes to starting the business. Labor in prayer and seek the face of God in order to find out what it is God has blessed you with that you already have enough of to bless you and your family.

Don't go trying to wear someone else's armor. Be who you are and do great work with what is in your hand. You've been at it for years. Maybe that is not what you wanted to do in life, but have you thought to seek God in why He caused you to spend so much time there? God asked Moses, "What's in your hand?" Moses replied, "A staff." In other words, Moses downgraded what he had right in his hands.

Your gift is just as important as the next person's gift. I know the other person's gift may seems glamorous and important. That may not be your grace that God has given you. Plus you don't know the weight that comes with being a glamorous star. The traveling it take never being at home. People pulling on you and draining you of what you have. Your specialty may be the Executive Protection for that start. You may be the stage manager that makes it all work. Your gift could be in the graphic design that makes that low self-esteemed person look like they have it all together.

The sowing skill that you were upset your mother made you learn could be the very skill that will dress the start and bring you in more income. Don't try to be someone else. Be who God made you to be. If God made you to be the best hair stylist, then style. If God created you to be the best long haul truck driver then do it great unto God and bring me my Amazon stuff. (My wife says I order too much on Amazon.) God may want to launch a laundry cleaner out of you because dirty cloths may be your pet peeve and you desire to start that business. Entre-PRAY-neur, be the best cloth cleaner out there and take care of God's great people.

Don't try to be something you are not. Don't disregard your gift because you are focused on what you see in someone else instead of what is right there on the inside of you. You are just as good as the next person and with the help of business trainers and focus groups you will be able to take your skill and use it for the kingdom of God in this dark world. Go and shine your light and let people know there is a better way.

PRINCIPLE:
Have more than one stream.

APPLICATION:
Monetize the different ways that you can use the same gift.

PRAYER:
Lord Jesus, I pray for the man or the woman reading this book right now. I pray that you will open their minds to how their gift can be used in different areas without stressing them out. Give them a specialized focus and expand their territory, Lord. In your name. Amen.

Finish It!
Chapter 10

1 Corinthians 9:24-27 (NIV)

²⁴ Do you not know that in a race all the runners run, but only one gets the prize? Run in such a way as to get the prize. ²⁵ Everyone who competes in the games goes into strict training. They do it to get a crown that will not last, but we do it to get a crown that will last forever. ²⁶ Therefore I do not run like someone running aimlessly; I do not fight like a boxer beating the air. ²⁷ No, I strike a blow to my body and make it my slave so that after I have preached to others, I myself will not be disqualified for the prize.

Isaiah 40:31 (NKJV)

³¹ But those who wait on the Lord shall renew their strength; They shall mount up with wings like eagles, They shall run and not be weary, They shall walk and not faint.

God did not make you to be a quitter. Finish it! Starting a business, or operating a business in such a dark world, being a Christian is not going to be easy, but God has not put more on you than you can bear. Finish it! Your kids are watching, God is expecting, people need what you have. Finish it! Don't talk yourself out of the vision that God has given you. Finish it!

As I close out this book I want you to know that you didn't start this race to quit. I remember seeing a video on Facebook where a young man was running a race and along the way for whatever reason his leg begin to actually cramp up. What was honorable about this young man and this race was that even in coming in dead last not just of this race but of the national and international time, he finished his race. He limped all the way to the finish line even to the point that his father who was in the stands jumped over the rail to come be by his side and assist him in finishing his race.

So no matter how hard it may get, keep your hands in God's hand. You have been built for this. There will be some valley experiences that go right alongside of the mountain top experiences. All of them are meant to assist you with the next phase of this business, life, or whatever, but finish it!

My team and I have strategized a broken-down step-by-step plan and course to be able to come along side you in your divine journey. You may or may not partner with us as we give you the pathway to get where God wants you to be but we are willing to jump out of the stands to come along side of you and assist you in starting as well as finishing your race.

The race that you are in right now is a race to know who you are and what gift God has purposed in your life that will change its trajectory. We have been in business long enough in a collaborative state that we have more than enough skill to help you. There are money holders near you that God has assigned for you to bring alongside to help you finish it. You are as smart, as strong, as disciplined as those you have around you.

Discipline is what it is going to take. Many people think that starting their own will give them more time to themselves and this ladies and gentleman is a myth. Owning our own business, especially one that God has assigned you to, will take more prayer then you are used to. Good by the way. You will have some late nights and some early mornings. I for instance have been up since 1:00 a.m. to complete these last two chapters in order to meet a deadline or get as close as I can.

Your eight-hour days will turn into fourteen-hour days. Your money will become funny. You will however work the plan, plant the seed, pave the path, take the risk, embrace the failures, and you will win. It is in your DNA. You are a kingdom child. Part of a chosen generation. Another Scripture that the world has turned cliché is Philippians 4:13 which says you can do all things through Christ Jesus which strengthens you. Well you can do all things through Christ.

Entre-PRAY-neur

This is what this is all about. Putting God first and allowing him to guide you to the finish line of the business he has created in you to bless His great people with. If not you, then who? God asked the question in Isaiah 6.

Isaiah 6:8 (NIV)
⁸ Then I heard the voice of the Lord saying, "Whom shall I send? And who will go for us?" And I said, "Here am I. Send me!"

Will you answer the call to start a business that God will use to bless His great people and show them Jesus in you? Can God Himself use you to be the beacon of light in a smog-filled world to bring His people safely to His throne? Answer yes. You can do it so I don't see why you wouldn't. Even though you can't see how, by faith it will manifest in your life because you trust and know that God will not call you to do something and not provide for you. Be obedient and say yes!

I love you and I know that you will be great. Send us some emails and let us know how you are doing. Let us know how we can help. Take the masterclass that is promoted in the next few pages. Allow me and the team to show you how to hear from God and launch out in the deep. You got this.

Father, in the name of Jesus I pray for each person reading this book, Lord. I say thank you for girding me up on every side and getting me to a point where I can help them. Now Lord, I speak blessing over their lives, businesses, families, and relationships. Cause your face to shine upon them and give them the vision to go out and bless Your great people. I pray this pray in the mighty name of Jesus. Amen (it is so).

PRINCIPLE:
Finish what you started.

APPLICATION:
Keep your eyes on the Lord and your ears open to hear the Lord.

PRAYER:
Lord Jesus, I pray for the man or the woman reading this book right now. I pray that you will give them the tenacity to finish. Show them the finish line and give them the power to run their race all the way to the end. If they are passing the baton at the end we pray for those who will receive it. In your name we pray. Amen.